The Art of Closure

By Lonnie Jones, Jr.

Published by TEAM PUBLICATIONS LLC

Brenda Hill, Editor-in-Chief

Champange, Editor

Tracy Clark, General Manager Lake Charles, LA 70605

Text ©2018 by Lonnie Jones, Jr.
Cover Art ©2018 Lonnie Jones, Jr.

Back Cover Photo Courtney Lynn O'Banion

Book Design: Vinh Alexander
www.vinhphotography.com

ISBN -13: 978-0-9969009-4-2

This book or parts thereof may not be reproduced in any form, stored in a retrieval system, or transmitted in any form by any means-electronic, mechanical, photocopy, recording, digital, or otherwise-without prior written permission of the author and illustrator, except as provided by United States of America copyright law.

Printed in the United States of America
Published in the United States of America

Unless otherwise indicated, scripture quotations are from the King James Version of the Bible.

Library of Congress Cataloging-in-Publication Data
Jones, Jr., Lonnie, 1985

The content in this book is for information purposes only, and not intended to diagnose or provide medical advice or take the place of a physician or therapist. Readers are advised to consult with qualified professionals regarding emotional conflict, depression, suicidal ideations, etc. The author nor publisher is responsible for any circumstances, consequences or happenings of anyone reading or following information in this book. If readers are on prescription medications, consult with your physician before stopping any medications.

Acknowledgments:

A special thanks to Pascha Gibson for introducing me to poetry and the true beauty of it.

To Matt and Victoria, who pushed me to enter my poems in different poetry contests.

To Tommy "Spaceman" Young for giving me the money to get the publication started, for buying the book I was published in, and forcing me to sign the page my poem was on.

To Lake Charles Memorial Outpatient Rehab, 'the one place,' where I obtained most of my inspiration for each poem.

I have learned so much from every person there. Over the years, this clinic has helped me grow tremendously as a person. Just to be around such an extremely supportive group of people is a true blessing.

This was 'the one place' that could alleviate my stressful thoughts since day one.

'The one place' where fellow employees, and even the patients recognized my full potential. I wish the entire staff nothing but the best. Thank you for the fond memories.

To My Goonies, family, and Facebook readers…

To God for putting only the right people in my life.

So many people have helped me along this journey.

Some have given me a place to stay, and some fed me when I had not eaten in weeks.

Dedication:

This book is dedicated

to my family, friends, and

my Godchildren...

Kayleigh, Jaxsen

and...

Journei N. Watts,
Sept. 13, 2016 - Sept. 19, 2016.

R.I.P.

"I never had the chance to hold you, but I promise to hold the precious memory of you."

Introduction

Within this private protective rib cage,

lies the feelings that could decorate any page.

In the middle compartment of my chest,

lies the vital essence of every emotion.

As it beats with no commotion,

it flows with great devotion.

It pumps passion through

the upper left and right atria;

and left and right ventricle.

It often ventures through

my typical emotional adventures,

with hopes of reaching a different pinnacle.

Various fluctuations of its value;

avoiding the tension, it often goes through.

If You're Reading This...

This is complete closure from,
my stressful times on this earth.
I have played back every stressful situation,
from my past to a mental re-birth.
A part of me felt cursed, as if
someone wanted to see me at my worse.
But as seconds, minutes, hours, days,
weeks, months, and years have passed,
I've figured out a way to mentally
relieve my stressful thoughts.
I don't know what the next person is
going through, so therefore I wrote this book.
If you're reading this, I just want
you to know I'm just like you.

Welcome to The Art of Closure...

I once accepted defeat, now I'm shaped by a past,
I have faith that these stressful days won't last.
I used to crave cars and clothes and even greed;
romance, love, and poetry are now my desired need.
Creativity sneaks up on me without a peep,
I've realized a great idea doesn't like to sleep.
My mind displays a future that is unseen,
weird dreams of me finding a noble queen.
I've released thoughts from my head,
because some things need to be said.
I have a lot of 'whys' as various emotions collide.
Memories of my cries, with thoughts of suicide.
I've sat back, carefully listened and observed,
preparing how food for thought would be served.
Creativity mixed with flashbacks that may come,
just to tell the truth about my life in this medium.
I struggle every day, but I can't let depression in,
I'm here to become better than I've ever been.

Everything is carefully understood,
everything is practiced in this selfhood.
Everything is about the person I wish I was,
everything I do is done without making a fuss.
Everything is used, pain, love and distrust,
everything is mentioned even a past I discussed.
Everything is everything, every moment is
defined by trying to make sense of everything.

I WELCOME YOU TO

THE ART OF CLOSURE...

Table of Contents

- Acknowledgments: 3
- Dedication: 5
- Introduction 6
- If You're Reading This... 7
- Welcome to The Art of Closure... 8
- ; 16
- Compathy: Session I 17
- Episode I 18
- The Aftermath I 20
- A Prayer Doused in Whiskey 22
- Episode II 24
- The Aftermath II 26
- The Apology (Intro) 28
- In the Heart of My Memory Archive 30
- Feeding Your Mental Appetite I 36
- A Scoash of Faith 37
- The Prayer 38
- Hevē Härt (Heavy Heart) 40
- From the Depths of Sorrow... 42
- The Lost Gentleman 46
- Change Your Regularly Scheduled Program 48

- ❀ Soul Searching in Depressing Waters 50
- ❀ The Change 52
- ❀ Compathy: Session II 54
- ❀ Feeding Your Mental Appetite II 56
- ❀ Diamond in the Rough 57
- ❀ In This Life You Lead 58
- ❀ Pity Party Reservation 59
- ❀ Episode III 60
- ❀ The Aftermath III 62
- ❀ Feeding Your Mental Appetite III 66
- ❀ Everything Happens for a Reason 67
- ❀ When in the Driver Seat 69
- ❀ Ignorance Is Not Bliss 70
- ❀ Compathy: Session III 72
- ❀ Story of my Life 74
- ❀ A Fool's Lust (2:58am) 77
- ❀ Untitled 79
- ❀ Finding the Right Tune 80
- ❀ Her Best Kept Secret 82
- ❀ N.I.G.G.A. 83
- ❀ Untitled Entry of Despair 85
- ❀ Untitled Entry of a Heart Break 87
- ❀ Resenting Artificial Love 90
- ❀ ... 92

- ❊ The Unknown Author   96
- ❊ The Stressful Interlude   100
- ❊ Envisaging Vignettes In a Cottage Cheese Ceiling   102
- ❊ The Hunger...   108
- ❊ Compathy: Session IV   109
- ❊ Trust Issues   111
- ❊ Deep In My Subconscious (Intro)   113
- ❊ Melatonin Chronicles I   114
- ❊ A Hopeful Broadcast   116
- ❊ Nothing Heard, Nothing Spoken   118
- ❊ When I'm Caught in the Drift   120
- ❊ All in all...   122
- ❊ From My End...   123
- ❊ The Bipolar Charge (Intro)   124
- ❊ Sober Underneath the LED Lights (In My Room)   126
- ❊ The Pregame (Introspection)   128
- ❊ Drunk Underneath The Flashing Lights (The Wharf)   130
- ❊ Episodes IV   132
- ❊ The Aftermath IV   134
- ❊ Feeding Your Mental Appetite IV   138
- ❊ True Beauty of Time   140
- ❊ Mark My Words   144
- ❊ Building Some Self-Confidence   145
- ❊ Meanwhile....   146

- ❀ To All Of The Poets....   147
- ❀ Mind Racing   148
- ❀ Downloading Heavenly Strength   154
- ❀ Give It to God   156
- ❀ Tuning In (Intro)   158
- ❀ Beats by Dre Effect   159
- ❀ A Grudge That Was Living Rent Free, Pt. I   160
- ❀ No Hidden Fees   162
- ❀ The Company I Keep   164
- ❀ 750mg of Honesty and a Proprietary Blend [750 mg of Honesty]   166
- ❀ [Proprietary Blend]   172
- ❀ Feeding Your Mental Appetite V   176
- ❀ So, Any Questions?   177
- ❀ My Practice   178
- ❀ Compathy: Session V   180
- ❀ Yearning for That Moment   182
- ❀ Cherishing the Fragmented Pieces   184
- ❀ A Portrait of Unity (Intro)   185
- ❀ Portrait of a Woman   186
- ❀ The Iris Effect   190
- ❀ Encore   191
- ❀ Wiping Away Her Tears...   192
- ❀ A Senseless Flower of Remembrance I   194
- ❀ Heart of Gold   196

- ❀ The Inception of a Beauteous Universe   199
- ❀ What Love May Bring…   200
- ❀ Can I Just Be Honest I   202
- ❀ A Senseless Flower of Remembrance II   204
- ❀ The Main Ingredient   206
- ❀ The Imaginings in My Head   208
- ❀ Queen of Hearts   209
- ❀ An Eyeful of Pulchritude (Intro)   210
- ❀ As I Admire Her Instagram Photos   211
- ❀ The Message I Want to Send   212
- ❀ Just a Moment of Your Time…   213
- ❀ iOS Love Update   214
- ❀ If You Ever Want Real Love…   216
- ❀ Hopefully One Day…   219
- ❀ The Mirror Dimension   222
- ❀ From: All Four Chambers To: Kayleigh & Jaxsen (My Godchildren)   230

A Conglomeration of Poems, While I Saved Up for My Publication Deposit…   235

- ❀ Pardon the Interruption with Twenty-One Minutes Left   243
- ❀ Anhedonia   244
- ❀ Melatonin Chronicles II   251
- ❀ Gin and Tonic with a Freshly Cut Lime   256
- ❀ Hidden Agenda   262

Notes   263

;

Depression can drift you
away like a leaf in the wind.
If you get caught in the drift;
this is not the end,
you are destined to win.
You could come across your destiny;
when facing a great deal of adversity.
With a large amount of the right curiosity,
could lead you toward your true identity.

Compathy: Session I

When moments of stress would
appear, I would have these urges
of wanting to disappear.
Part of it was fear along with
other situations, I'd rather not
mention at this time.
Anyway, I just wanted to
get away, die in my sleep or
get in a car accident and fade away.
Hell, I even had potent thoughts
of me taking my own life.
But I faced the fact,
that no one told me to give up.
At that moment, I stared in the mirror
and acknowledged my every flaw.
And… That's when the journey of me
changing; trying to find the true me.
I went from wanting to take my own life,
to wanting to find my worth on this earth.

Episode 1

Clouded mind with perception,
half empty bottle, hankering more.
Stressful tears soaking this carpet floor,
whiskey burning my inner core.
Clasping, squeezing my hands,
trying to bare this weight.
Nose to the floor, chin in my
chest, losing my faith.
Voluminous flow of thoughts
has my heart in a figure eight.
Leftover thoughts buried underneath
the present thoughts on this plate.
If I could only take a brief
of relief from this disbelief.
Trying to climb myself out of this pit
of self-pity.
Will I reach the top with relief?
Suicidal thoughts begin to flow fluidly.
Will these thoughts ever cease?

Thoughts begin to deceive me,
convincing me this will give me peace.
My train of thought is now
clouding my self-esteem mentally.
Trying to get off this page, making an
issue of various emotions and my identity.
I'm losing my grip, taking another willing sip,
this can't be a part of my destiny.
Lord give the serenity, help me get
rid of this suicidal tendency.
Tussling with this depression,
trying to avoid the aggression.
I close my eyes, searching for an exit,
looking for another mental intersection....
To be continued....

The Aftermath I

Time and time again, I think about that
phone call I received at 5 a.m.
The tears that fell during
my mid-term, the loss of
sleep, and the excessive drinking.
It was like everything
around me was crumbling.
Hearing about my parents
splitting up, brought out
a different part of me.
Here's where I didn't care
about going to class.
I didn't want to go
home for the holidays.
I even ignored everyone's
phone call.

A Prayer Doused in Whiskey

I can't shake this feeling away from me,
drinking this whiskey as if it's only the key.

Unlocking more doors of frustration,
everyone's concerned about my situation.

I've been isolating myself, skipping class,
spending my last on liquor,
and I'm always mad.

My girlfriend keeps calling,
she thinks I'm cheating.

Music blasting trying to defer my
suicidal thoughts, but my
situation plays on repeat.

I get on my knees, begging the Lord please;
put my mind at ease, PLEASE...

Get rid of these thoughts that stampede.

Why does this have to happen to me?
Why can't I move forward with Godspeed?

Dear Heavenly Father, WHY, WHY, WHY?...

Why does this pain have to be mine?
I try, I try, I try, please ease my mind!

I never asked for this, I beg of you.
Just get my mind, body,
and soul out of this bind.

Episode II

A whiskey bottle gripped firmly,
I take a few swigs with no hesitation.
I'm still looking for that mental intersection…

As I sit in this room alone
avoiding everyone's attention.
I feel the corruption from this mental infection,
I can't stay focused; no sense of direction.

No longer a connection with my girlfriend;
I've been avoiding her affection.
Inadequate amount of motivation;
I need some correction.

In this lonely session of introspection
with no sound reflection.
With objections of trying to elude
the subjection of this depression.

A part of me knows the way out,

the other part sees the deception.

I cry out to God to give me

some type of mental protection.

I can't fight this feeling, now I'm in the

mirror staring deeply in to my reflection.

The Aftermath II

Each day was a constant struggle,
my girlfriend finally gave up on me.
When we broke up, I felt nothing.
I just wanted to be alone.

My friends did their best
to keep my mind occupied.

They took me to different bars,
clubs, and sometimes parties.
They really displayed true friendship.
I gave them a glimpse of the old me at times.

The only problem was, they weren't always
around, they had to go to class most of the time.

Those times I was alone, I felt detached
from reality, I often searched for meaning.

As apathy was setting in, a young woman I was
close friends with confessed her love for me.

I never realized this until now, I was using her…
Yes, I had feelings for her, but I couldn't
shake this feeling I was battling.

She was a friend with strong benefits,
but she deserved someone better than me.
There were moments, where she
really made me feel alive.

In the long run I broke her heart…

The Apology (Intro)

I gave up on everything, including love and even God. I let you down, I gave you the worst of me instead of giving you the best of me. Till this day, I still play back everything, I feel the regret. I'm sorry, I wish I could undo everything and give you everything.

In the Heart of My Memory Archive

I nonchalantly scroll down.
I see a picture of you in my news feed.
I'm caught in a drift of the
time when I felt so alive.
My heart still remembers
those feelings I had for you.
My mind remembers
everything I admired about you.
Every detail of your smile,
even the sound of your laugh.
Reflecting on the time,
I once felt complete.
The time we were together,
you tried to calm me through
the emotional weather.
Let's face it... It's my fault.
I pushed you away.

I never wanted to hurt you, but I
ended up doing it anyway.
After letting you slip through my fingers…
I had to stop being who I was,
some changes needed to be made.

Excuse me… As I avoid these tears;
I've eluded these thoughts for years.
This is probably why love is one of my fears.
This change was all for you…
Or someone that was similar to you…
Every day I think about that day…
I wish, I could go back and
change it in every way.

Still till this day, I sometimes
read over the old text messages.

Now that I've overcome
depression and other emotions,
I've realized life would've been easier,
if I would've never pushed you away.
Over the years curiosity has killed me slowly.

I play back every moment, I've cherished with you.
I would daydream of us in my spare time.
I picture all the places we never visited.
All the texts that were never sent;
all the words we never spoke.
The wedding we should have had,
the kids we could have had.
Time we never shared,
I wish I could rewind the past.

At the time you were healing,
I wanted to call, just to verbalize...I love you.
But I didn't, I would have been
playing with your emotions.

A selfish act just to keep you near,
when I didn't even know myself.
After letting you slip through my fingers,
I had to stop being who I was.
Some changes needed to be made.

I've eluded these thoughts for years.
This is probably why love is one of my fears.
This change was all for you...
Or someone that was similar to you...
Every day I think about that day...
I wish, I could go back and
change it in every way.

Back then I would look
at your profile, just to see
if your status changed.
Imagining myself in
every profile picture with you.

I know you and I
are history. I never
wanted to get in the way.

Every day I bear it all,
at the end of day, I know
who I was born to be all along.
If you read each poem,
you'll notice some of
my privacy is gone.
I don't need shelter from
the downpour.
I know exactly
what I was built for.
If I ever meet someone
like you again; I promise
to hold on tight this time.

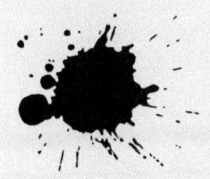

From time to time, I do my best
not to fantasize about you.
There are times, I wish you were
here to tame these thoughts.
As you slay this savage beast
of stress with your presence.
Healing me with your touch,
curing me with your kiss.

Feeding Your Mental Appetite I

You must lose something,
In order to gain something.
So, losing yourself is the
cost of finding yourself.

A Scoash of Faith

I couldn't keep my grades up,
plus, I kept skipping class.
I was placed under academic probation,
I was still caught in this emotional war.
I let her move on with her life,
even though I had a deep love for her.
I couldn't drag her along this emotional
roller coaster that has no sense of thrill.
I moved back to a home that was broken,
my parents tried to stay together.
I could feel the negative
tension throughout the house.
I got a job and played a lot of basketball,
because I didn't want to be at home.
One night I decided to put my
faith in the Lord one more time,
so, I got on my knees to pray.

The Prayer

Dear Heavenly Father,
I come to you because there is
so much going on in my life,
I need some guidance.
I can't function without having
some type of adulterated beverage.
Thoughts of me taking my own life still lingers.
I ask you to change me as a person.
Give me the ability to speak fluidly;
I'm so tired of stuttering.
Give me the wisdom and knowledge
to overcome any problem.
Equip me with motivation
and dedication
to accomplish any
goal I set for myself.

Hevē Härt (Heavy Heart)

Marinated in depression,
sprinkled with a scour of jealousy.
Preheated for self-destruction,
baked in a high temperature of self-pity.
Slowly cooked by hypertension,
avoiding extra salt from this reality.
Lies, broken promises, heart breaks,
and various problems, increasing my animosity.
Vandalized by this world and my own thoughts,
trying to improve my emotional density.
With every thought I get sentimental,
uncertain outcomes alongside this anxiety.
Notoriously insecure, equipping my
heart with a pad lock for security.
Looking for a life with better emotional
benefits, trying to create a different recipe.

Craving for a second chance, making
dinner reservations with destiny.
Stopping the amount of hatred
in my heart with no penalty.
Channeling every emotion from my heart,
into a ridiculous amount of honesty.
Confidence could give me emotional
stability, and a long period of prosperity.
Blood flowing through my atria and
ventricle with a conglomeration of serenity.
With every poem it will send a four-part harmony,
creative melodies with longevity.
Every life line opens chambers
of development with a superior
quality of durability.
Quantity of pain was born here,
it will not die here; here's where
love basks with great potency.

From the Depths of Sorrow...

Look deeply in my eyes, and
see a fellow that's trapped in his own mind.

Look deep inside my mind as these
thoughts execute a strong stride.
Look deeper inside as exhilaration
and anxiety begin to collide.

This is why, I often avoid eye contact,
pretending like everything is fine.
Fake smiles while anguish flows fluidly
beneath my skin, causing me to hide.

As my confidence decline,
could explain why my love is so blind.

Depression loves my company,
it never takes the time to compromise.

This vicissitude is something I can't change,
I must use my precious time just to improvise.

Love and hatred sometimes combine,
avoiding impulses that jealousy can provide.

Stop this whining, survive, grow a pair,
and leave this depression behind.

I must be hard on myself till I'm satisfied,
make sure my courage can't be falsified.

Here's where I decide to rise from the depths
of sorrow and claim a life that is mine.

At the end of the day,
I'm just a lost adventurer.
Searching for the hidden
treasures of life...

The Lost Gentleman

I used to stare inside of a whiskey glass,
trying to see this life that I live a lot clearer;
reoccurring events, emotions rising, clinching this sink,
staring into the mirror,
steady tears falling, crying myself a river,
self-destructing voyage, destroying my liver.

I'm becoming more emotional on this liquor, expiring
fortitude, requiring a different attitude.
Looking into the clouds, scouring for a silver lining,
wondering if my pain can be inspiring.
Symbolizing a gentleman with different wiring, focusing
on ways to be more aspiring.
Trying to give love a good name; how can I think of
love, when my pain needs to be tamed.

Dreaming of a woman in designer clothes, painting a
fresh coat of love, healing my heart.

Waking up from my lucid dream, envisaging vignettes in a cottage cheese ceiling.
Issues indenting deeply inside my mentality, searching for grit that lay deeply inside of me.
Issues with identifying who I am, who I don't want to be, who I want to be, who I need to be.

Now I'm admiring this mirror, focusing on my flaws, preparing myself to face reality.
Retiring this cowardly feeling, avoiding the clashing of my negative personality.
Taking a deep breath, holding this confident feeling, sculpting a man with a better personality.

Change Your Regularly Scheduled Program

Life can be filled with unscripted seasons of ill-advised emotional episodes along with commercials of stress. Write your own script carefully and honestly, be the star character. Be the hero of your own story and never let anyone condense or alter your script, not even Hollywood.

Soul Searching in Depressing Waters

Flowing through an ocean of emotions,
scouring for different motives,
avoiding tidal waves, sailing through
life with many objectives,
clouds of despair form.
Desolate mizzle with flashes of anxiety
in the eye of the brain storm,
stressful winds of forty-eight knots,
taking the course of action
through waves of an emotional tide.
In the heart of the sea, trying to
elude the Depression Triangle,
this triangle has been known to
make vessels of confidence disappear.
Without warning a rogue wave climbs
to 23 feet, knocking over my vessel.

Without my vessel of confidence,
it's just me and a raft of little faith.
Floating in this ocean of emotions,
as the clouds of despair diminish,
I begin to feel the radiant rays
from the sun, as it shines on me.
The calm after this storm gives
me a euphoric sense of courage.
It gives me innovation to build
a stronger vessel of confidence.

The Change

After my prayer, a part of me wanted
that change to happen overnight.
I knew better than that,
my mom always told me,
"You can't just pray to God and
expect him to do all of the work.
You have to put forth the effort
and he'll help you along the way."

So, I took the initiative to put forth
the effort. I started with getting
the word of the day, to the best
of my ability I would try to
pronounce it correctly.
I remember my speech therapist
telling me to take my time when I speak.
I remember using the mirror, to
help me pronounce certain words.

Till this day I remember my
first word of the day "acrimonious"
This was the start of a new me...

I wanted to lose weight;
I gained a lot while I was in college.
So... In order to gain the motivation
and the dedication I prayed
for; I knew I had to put forth the
effort to lose weight to create a better me.
Well the other part of me wanted to gain wisdom
and knowledge.
I felt like I just had to live life as much
as I could in a positive way.

Compathy: Session II

As I went through this metamorphosis
or as you have it "change," I realized
that I knew nothing about myself.
My parents still weren't together,
I still didn't believe in love.
I stayed home for a while,
I kept getting the word of
the day. Plus, I lost 40 pounds or so,
but I didn't know what I would do
with my life. I just didn't know.
My main focus was just to change myself.

One day my dad and I got in to
a pretty heated argument.
Somehow opportunity presented
itself for me to leave, and move to
Shreveport. Here's where another
chapter of my life began,

to prove to my dad that I am somebody.

Here's where I found out so
much about myself; how weak I was
emotionally, how ignorant I was,
how much of a sucker I was for love,
how much I realized I was pretending
to be someone else. But somehow
Shreveport is where I found myself,
and where I also discovered a
new friend called Poetry…

Feeding Your Mental Appetite II

If you're tired of the consistency of drama, then stray away from that negative lifestyle or energy. Stop having these intentions of pretending to be someone you are not and be who you are. Stop surrounding yourself with meaningless ignorance and surround yourself with priceless wisdom.

Diamond in the Rough

Disadvantaged environment, trapped in the rough,
Unrecognizable for my value when I'm in my raw stage.
I wonder if I have the potential to be more.
I wish I was provided with an opportunity to shine.
All my days are tough, soaked in an emotional soil.
I'm obscured, take time out to notice my clarity.
My hidden talents have yet to be tamed.
My value has been shaded with doubt.
Should I wait for someone, to recognize this precious stones development?
No.... I must attempt to find and harness every emotion, stay positive, utilize my gifts.
With exerting great encouraging necessary efforts,
I could truly illuminate, once I reach my true potential,
while helping true rare gems shine.
But before I shine,
I have to be polished first.

In This Life You Lead

No matter how respectful you live your life,
Some will judge and disrespect you...
Probably because they weren't raised correctly,
or they don't want to understand you.
Some will try to crush your dreams...
Probably because they're afraid to dream,
or they don't want to see you succeed.
Some will steer you in the wrong direction...
No matter what you do,
some will find a way to bring you down.
In this life you lead, learn how to treat people
the way you want to be treated.
Some will treat you badly,
just how others have treated them.
But you have the ability to break the cycle...
The only race to worry about
is the human race.

Pity Party Reservation

There will be parties only you can attend. It's up to you to let someone be your designated driver, to guide you home safely while helping you get over the emotional hangover.

Episode III

Living life with the best of my ability,
while trying to discover tranquility.
So much on my shoulders, is happiness
on my timeline, am I even getting closer.
Musing on the problems I'm facing;
I don't have a dream that's worth chasing.
What are my goals in life; I don't want to
work two jobs for the rest of my life.
I feel different since depression was pushed aside.
But, now I have other feelings bottled up inside.
I'm losing my patience.
I quite often get lost in a pit of self-pity of darkness.
I feel awful, awkward, I don't care if I seem heartless.
I feel atrocious, my ignorance is getting enormous,
no one has noticed, I've been losing my focus.
This negative energy stayed, preserved alongside
two free reserved middle fingers, with a few F bombs.
Clear as day with no subtitles...

The Aftermath III

I lived in Shreveport
for quite a few years.
I started talking to my mom again.
When I left I fell out of contact
with people in Lake Charles.
I wanted to avoid the questions of
"How are you doing?" "How's it going?"
and "How are you feeling?"
I felt ashamed when someone
asked those questions. I just felt weird.
Anyway, I worked two jobs,
I got the second job to help
my mom with her bills and my little
brother; who was three at the time.
All in all, I thought I could handle the
weight of trying to take care of
my mom and my little brother.
I was wrong…One day I just broke down

crying, I realized I was going nowhere fast.
I was a starving artist and that's all.
I didn't know where my life was going.
At that moment I felt empty, off balance,
with so much bottled up inside.
I realized everything that was
revolving around me and I asked myself,
"What am I destined for?"
"What is my sole purpose?"
Then a coworker introduced
me to poetry.
Here is where I learned so much about
myself and the beauty of things around me.
The most important thing is,
I had to be honest with myself and use my pain
to sculpt a better me.

When I first began writing poetry,
I didn't understand the concept.
My honesty was something
I wanted to keep to myself.
Many have read my every thought
from my past and present.
I often question my future
pessimistic thoughts along
with optimistic steps forward.
I often search for likes,
wondering if it could
make me feel successful.
But my main concern now is,
"Can I alleviate your stress with the pain of my past?"
If I plant the seed of relief, will it give you
opportunity to grow?

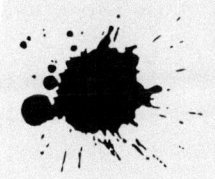

I often search for words.
There are so many words in the English language.
When I write a poem,
variations of words come to mind.
But I often get upset,
because I can't use them all.
After every poem I finish,
another word comes to mind;
I realize I could've used it.
Then I realize the beauty of poetry,
the beauty of the human mind.

Feeding Your Mental Appetite III

No matter what, in some situations your mental drive, confidence, motivation, any and every positive emotion that may lay dormant within you, will be tested.

Everything Happens for a Reason

We're all born to be great.
There must be trials and tribulations
alongside certain other situations.
These situations occur to help us
unlock the sizable magnitude of
greatness that lie within us.

For some, it's easy for them to talk confident,
but some of them find it hard to demonstrate it....

When in the Driver Seat

Some can be on the road of success;
even happiness and still manage
to get distracted by texting and driving,
instead of observing their surroundings…

Ignorance Is Not Bliss

As I live this life, I will be the man
always searching for answers.

Some rather swim in
an ocean current of ignorance.
Me! Well...I'd rather take the time to
understand each situation.

In order to spread love;
I must love myself.
Take a moment to understand
every walk of life is different.
Step back for just a second and
think about the different types
of pain, stress and different situations.
If there is a different ethnicity; put
myself in their shoes.
Imagine myself in their skin color,
then count my blessings.

Some people endure so much.
In the back of their minds.
Animosity is growing strong.

That's why I observe a person's
body language before I speak.
No matter what, my first impression
will be to make you laugh or smile.

A person with complete
understanding will not be perfect,
but they know what
positive buttons to push.

At the end of the day ignorance
is 'not' bliss, even the smartest
person can be ignorant.

Compathy: Session III

I just want to make a positive
impact in every way possible.
Like the people sent by God to
make a positive impact on me.

Secretly I search for a
significant other that can
have an impact on my life.

You see, I'm powered by
negative emotion.

I want to be enhanced by love.
Negative emotions can only
take you so far; when love
can take you above and beyond.

I often sit to myself and listen
to my heart.
Then I envision resting my forehead against
hers, showing her my vision.
A vision showing her a mission
to keep her out of an emotional prison.
My love will never be questioned,
actions will let her know.
I've made a firm decision!
No matter what kind of
bad position I'm in, I still
will take time out to
give her my undivided attention.

Story of my Life

When you want to give her
your undivided attention,
but the undivided attention that
you wanted to give is divided.

She'd rather give her undivided
attention to someone else.

But when you give another woman
your undivided attention,
she adds herself to the equation
and gracefully demands your
undivided attention.

It's easy for me to confab
with any woman; when it comes
to being around a potential woman I like.
It's hard for me to ask her out, and, etc…
I sometimes feel like I know the answer…
One side of me wants to blame the world,
for imprinting that some must have certain
qualifications, standards and expectations
to receive, feel, and even to fall in love.
The other side knows I'm the one to blame,
for not having confidence in myself.
I'm done with trying to fit in,
it's time for me to stand out.
Money does not and did not mold me,
pain, struggle, and heartaches did;
along with strength and love,
holding me together.

If I confessed my love
would you believe me?

A Fool's Lust (2:58am)

He was recently admiring a picture
of her, taking in every single detail.
He spends his night tossing and turning,
through scenarios that may never come true.

Thoughts begin to grow stronger,
thoughts of he, thoughts of she,
thoughts of them being together,
wishing this could happen in reality.
Thoughts of her personality and
her heart at its full potential.
He wishes for one chance; he's ready
to start off moving forward amicably.

In all honesty, he tends to think about his past,
and begins to feel like a fool, lusting for
something that's not genuine anymore.
He's so obsessed with wanting to experience,
the love that first Corinthians speaks of.

I feel the affection of her emotions,
its makes me feel alive.
Heavy heart of stone,
she sculpts me from the inside.
When anguish and anxiety collide,
her love makes everything fine.
She shows me what love can provide,
when my confidence begins to decline.
I give her more reason to be mine,
because my love can't be falsified.

Untitled

I envisage about you and I...
When you laugh or smile;
scenarios begin to pile.

Your low-maintenance;
maintaining my patience.
Guidance thru your true essence;
a work of art with great balance.

Don't care what people think of us;
grateful if you accept my love.
If I ever had a chance to love,
I would want it to be with you.

Finding the Right Tune

Kisses connecting us on the same frequency,
I'm well alarmed of her erogenous areas.
I rather connect the flow of our four chambers.
Connecting two hearts, enticed in a figure eight.
Her love is always cherished in these arms.
Caressing her skin, fingers moving as if
I was playing chords on a guitar.
My hands in rhythm with every curve,
smoothing out her mental rough edges.
I appreciate her love like a rich note
from a beautiful soulful song.
When she's emotionally wounded,
I'll give her my love, when things
in her life go wrong.

Why did you push me away?...
I was always full of good intentions...
I understand you're not perfect...
I understand you wanted to work on yourself...
I wanted to be around to witness your growth...
I wanted to be around when you finally found yourself.

Her Best Kept Secret

She never told anyone about us;
not even a peep about the love we shared.
Afraid of what her family would say.
She feared their disappointments,
their threats.
We could never display our love in public.
She was afraid that someone might find out.
Our love was only shown behind
closed doors.
I often felt like she was ashamed of our love.
I've given her so much of my love,
I was afraid of letting her go.
The moment I felt valueless,
I knew I had to let her go.
I hated feeling that way,
along with being her best kept secret.
I was the right man for her,
just not the right color.

N.I.G.G.A.

Never judged by my personality or my actions.

Ignorant people don't want to understand me.

Getting animosity for the way God created me.

Goals to achieve greatness, spread love and share creativity.

Accomplished poet that wants to be accepted for who I am.

I know, I'm not the
person you want me to be…
But…I'm the person I need to be…

Untitled Entry of Despair

After you cheated on me,
I often blamed myself.
I've always paid attention to your needs.
For some reason a part of me wanted to
give you another chance.
It was only, because I felt like...
I will never find anyone else as good you.

As if you were as good as it gets.
I was wrong,
I've realized I did everything right.
You wanted someone
that paid attention
to your wants.

I know, I will never find
anyone else as good as you.
I'm for sure, I will find
someone better than you.

Love once stared her in the face
with every chance it had, but it never
took the courage to acknowledge itself.
Instead it only witnessed the effects
of her getting engaged to someone else.

Untitled Entry of a Heart Break

He wanted to redefine love,
show her what commitment is.
A few inquiries to know her likes,
dislikes and her interests.
He tries not to ogle over her assets,
he admires her personality.

Half of him wants to stay single,
the other half wants to settle down.
Hope begins to build higher,
faith begins to grow stronger.
Thoughts of her are posted
on his mental cork board.
His interest has him anxious
to spend time with her.
His excitement rejuvenates him,
it gives him more reason.

He always finds ways
to make her smile.
He wants her to feel as
special as he feels.

As things move smoothly,
the tables turn without warning.
She begins to become distant,
he senses her lack of interest.
With every text message,
he begins to feel the distance.
Losing sleep night after night,
re-evaluating the situation.

He comes across her in public,
his stomach quivers.
He begins to feel embarrassed,
trying not to make eye contact.
She gives him a mild look,
then quickly looks down.

What did he do wrong?
What didn't he do?
Judging his own identity,
judging the way he dresses.
Nitpicking his personality,
his flaws, his habits.

Hope begins to decline dramatically,
faith begins to grow mild.

Trying different activities
to shake this feeling.
Every woman begins to
look similar to her.
Wishing he could select and
cut this episode.

Instead she's just a stranger
he used to know.

Resenting Artificial Love

Why do you only notice me,
now that I'm gone?

Why couldn't you forget
about the meaningless
materialistic things
that revolved around you?

You never cherished every
moment we spent together.
I gave you all of me, but
I received nothing in return.

You had a good man,
but never took the time
to learn how to treat him.

So many late-night messages
of "I'm sorry" and "I miss you."

I gave in just to re-establish
only our friendship and
nothing more.
I made that clear.
You only stayed around
for a few weeks, waiting
for signs that means that
I forgive you and we can start over.

...

Why...
Am I thinking about you?...
You and I are through,
but I think about you
through and through.

I used to wait for that day,
there's nothing else to say.
I've always searched
for a different way.
Maybe, I'm running out
of complete sentences
and phrases to say.

Really, I wish I had my way...

Why...
Am I thinking of
your body and face?
Why am I feeling like this?
You're the one thought
I want to replace.
Often my heart hungers
for that emotional taste.

Should I shed light
from a different height?

Some nights I fight
with all my might.
I need some insight,
no exit in sight,
but it feels right.

Why...

Am I thinking of your touch?

You were such a stress reliever.

So much of an emotional healer,

but you fell out of touch.

These thoughts are running

through my mind.

Our love is lost, It's something

I don't want to find.

I don't want any explanation,

it will be a waste of my time.

I realize I don't want to lose

myself trying to love you.

I've noticed money can get in the way of cupid's arrow.

The Unknown Author

She walks into a book store,
not knowing what kind of book she's looking for.

She carefully walks each aisle.
The last few books that she read,
started off with a good plot.
It had her attention for a few chapters,
but ended terribly.

She continues to walk each aisle.
She reaches the last aisle,
notices a black hardback book.
It sits on the shelf all alone and lonesome.
She wonders why it's placed in the dark corner.

She kind of judges it by its cover,
she's clueless about why it doesn't
have a colorful cover that stands out.

No title, the spine text seems like
it has been crossed out, the back
blurb catches her attention.

After carefully examining the book,
she opens it and sees the author's name.
The title page inside and the table
of contents catches her interest.
Curiosity begins to increase, she sits
down and begins skimming over
chapter one and two.

Losing track of time, she begins
to get drawn into each chapter.
Takes it home for a little alone time,
and maybe with a glass of wine.

Some chapters make her cry,
some make her laugh and fill her with joy.
Wondering what's going to happen next,
and why she hasn't come across
this kind of book before.

Finds herself ardent after each chapter,
she falls asleep with the book in her arms.

Tells her family and friends about
this book and how great it is so far.
Tells them where she found it,
and how happy she is about finding it.

She doesn't care what others think of the cover,
the book makes her feel whole.

Never letting it go, never wanting it to end,
never letting anyone else read her copy.

She realizes that it's not all
about the title of the book.
It's what the book
has to offer inside.

That's what counts!
Every author has a story,
but will you take the time
to open up,
and understand it?

The Stressful Interlude

Sitting in this apartment full of darkness,
slowly becoming heartless.
I shouldn't get back my deposit.
Over the past four months my tears have
stained this carpet.
Waiting for a call back from
the application I submitted at Target.

There's an eviction notice,
plus, I'm really starving.
I feel light headed, and I'm even
starting to get really nauseous.
Opening and closing these cabinets
making all kinds of commotion.

Asking God to take my life away.
I can't get a handle on these emotions.
Nothing else to burn in my stomach,
I fall to the floor trying to regain my focus.

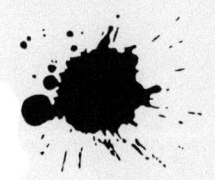

Loneliness has been eating me alive...

Envisaging Vignettes In a Cottage Cheese Ceiling

Another day of coming to an
apartment with no electricity.
Artificial light shining through
the blinds, I can see some of
these dark areas clearly.
Hard to believe, I'm still living
this way. Feels like this is all my fault.

Switching my iPhone to vibrate
for a moment, I just need some privacy.
Drinking an adulterated beverage,
trying to alter this current mood.
Lying in bed, hands behind my
head, searching for tranquility.
Deep breaths, trying to relax,
closing my eyes scouring for ataraxia.

Clusters of problems clouding
my judgement, driven to despair.
Trying to cancel these appointments
of being weak for a minute.
Grabbing my phone, pressing the
home button, checking the battery life.
Sliding my thumb up, turning down the
brightness, then turning on the light.

Placing my iPhone face down on my
chest, illuminating one side of the room.
Focusing my sights on this cottage
cheese ceiling, still scouring for this feeling.
Closing my eyes, trying to begin a quiet
introspection of this scrambled mind.
In through the nose, out through the mouth,
thinking of a place other than Louisiana.

Eluding where the past dwelt, trying
to eschew from certain thought bubbles.
I open my eyes and begin to see this
cottage cheese ceiling take shape.
An evocative episode begins fading
into the ceiling without a definite border.
It shows me being comfortable with
a passionate significant other.

Cuddling, spooning out a scoop
of her love, holding her hand gently.
She clinches my hand tightly, verbalizing
her feelings in a smooth mellifluous tone.
I begin to physically feel, fluttering
butterflies in my stomach.
Resuming this evocative episode,
now I'm absorbing her bouncy personality.

Face to face, this is the perfect time
and place, exchanging positive vibes.
I can smell the sweet aroma of truth,
exhaling vapors of true love.
I'm beginning to feel ataraxy through
each vignette in this ceiling.
This vignette displays me being confident,
able to withstand any situation.

She increases my determination,
giving me more reason to move forward.
Always making me smile, always by
my side when I need her.
Friendship, partnership sets the
tone of this magnificent relationship.
A strong firm of love built on trust, and
support with an unbreakable connection.

Without any caution, this evocative
episode begins to whirl inward.
The ceiling begins to shake, I'm woken
by a phone vibrating on my chest.
Sitting upright in bed, checking my
phone to see whose calling me.
Trying to collect my thoughts from
this dream within a dream.

Photographically memorizing a
woman with eyes that shines like pearls,
with an angelic show stopping smile,
along with honey sweet kissable lips.
She was beauteous in sweats or
in designer clothes.
I can only imagine the experience
from this type of woman.

I don't want to bore any woman
with my troubles.
I struggle every day, but these dreams
help me make it through the night.
Dreams of success, love and a life with
little stress could make me feel complete.
Maybe she's out there, maybe she
will accept me for who I am.

Maybe I'll get to know true love,
maybe we could help each other
rise above any situation.
Maybe time will tell, who knows.......

The Hunger...

Starving artist striving to feed this wishful
appetite, but confidence is losing weight.

Ambulating at a slow rate,
with every step, I'm losing faith.

Negative emotions dampen my enthusiasm,
I'm questioning my personality trait.
The feeling of worthlessness creating hate,
while debt collectors call and give me a date.
Mysterious sparks of inspiration and a past
are the reasons I stay awake.
Working two jobs with a lack of motivation,
I'm always arriving late.

Often, I search for strength,
and guidance in a dwelling place.
It always feels like I'm against all odds,
but giving up would be my biggest mistake.

Compathy: Session IV

Years ago, I was extremely
scared of being lonely.

As the years have passed,
I've really gotten numb to that particular feeling.

The more I draw from my current retrospection,
it reminds me of how lonely I am.
I've done everything by myself…
No physical presence by my side
to experience this transformation.

But at the end of the day
I've realized, I'm afraid of letting
someone in and getting hurt.
I already have enough
heartbreaks as it is.
Don't get me wrong, I really
want to let someone in.

The best part I remember about love is...
Being ardent to see my significant other.
Thinking of different outlandish
comments that will make her
laugh/smile while I wait.
Taking mental notes of her likes and dislikes.
Reviewing mental pictures of her body
language from my photographic memory.
Comforting her when she feels out of
place or when she needs to vent.
Giving her my undivided attention, then
adding in my two-cents; to
help her make sense of things.
Just overall being spontaneous...
I can write/verbalize about this
on so many levels, but this was a
random thought from out the blue.

Trust Issues

The human mind can embrace levels of romance that may bloom, but memories of past bad relationships can corrupt the positivity of those thoughts.

When I sleep, my subconscious displays me getting married, and having kids of my own. Then, I wake up with other wonders/questions about this life I live.

Deep In My Subconscious (Intro)

Sometimes I have to take melatonin;
my mind tends to race at night.

I think of all sorts of things,
from my past heartbreaks,
to a certain woman
I would love to be with.

I find it quite fascinating
how easy it is to verbalize,
how I don't believe in love.
But when I finally go to sleep my
subconscious shows me otherwise.

Melatonin Chronicles I

We both search for the truth;
if we expose the real me and you.
Would this be the right thing to do?

If we were to drop our guards;
would we finally have the room,
for a fresh flower of love to bloom?

Right now, it's just me and you.
As I embrace you in my arms,
I begin to feel a reaction.
I'm convinced that our hearts
have something to prove.

I'm done with being afraid
of letting someone in,
here's where I give in.
I'm ready to give it my all.
Are you ready to give it your all?
We're in this together,
so let's complete each other.
Here's where we build
something that will last.

A Hopeful Broadcast

I used to wish I could sleep forever;
I wish there was a mental lever.
I can put together dreams of success,
and a love that will last forever.

Even repeat different positive
situations over and over forever.

Accomplish the goals I've set for myself,
even control the Louisiana weather.

As my writing gets better and better,
will I ever be known for being clever?
A great poet with endeavors
of being the New Times Best Seller...

Nothing Heard, Nothing Spoken

I hear, "I'm not a morning
person," almost every day.
Lately I've been hearing,
"Your awfully quiet today."
If they only knew what
thoughts are at bay.

Life's a beach grab a sea
shell and lend me your ears.
Conglomeration of ideas with a
variety of disappointing fears.
As the sociable attitude disappears,
slowly anti-social appears.

Streams of confidential thoughts
that could diminish my potential.
I'm a quiet individual that
doesn't want to be identical.

I want to be an intelligent gent
with a handful of common sense.
I want to dish out food for
thought with a common scent.

A brew of depression and despair,
was sometimes my common scent.

My fears will only hold me back,
my tears won't bring me back.
I must keep my mental state intact,
improve the characteristic traits I lack.
Then I may have the possibilities
of a potent positive poet pouring it all out.

Until then I gather the pieces
from a man that was once broken.
This is the creative silence of what
I call nothing heard, nothing spoken.

When I'm Caught in the Drift

I realize to write with raw emotion;
I must reenact an event from the past.
Free falling deeply in to each thought,
taking my time to use each feeling wisely.

Sometimes, I get caught in this emotional wave.
Love tends to encourage me to think
about certain women I've loved before.
Stress reminds me how far
I've come emotionally.

On the outside something seems wrong.
On the inside, I'm on an emotional journey.
Sometimes I can control it, sometimes I can't...
I drift off at home, work, even when
I'm driving, some think I'm in a bad mood.
I get really quiet, with a deadpan look...
This only happens when I'm caught in the drift.

Exploring every feeling in the depths of my soul.

Here's where I've learned,
every life experience can be a poem.
Some streams of thoughts I try to avoid...

Lately, I've been gaining the confidence to explore.
Now if you would, excuse me as I begin to drift off.

All in all...

All kinds of emotions always
end up, all over the place.
All the way deep down inside,
I have no intentions to stop at all.

In all honesty, I'm all for giving
poetry an all-out effort.
One of my goals is to give
this life my all, till it's all over.

In order to achieve all around
greatness, it will all start with me.
If I give all my all, will it display
the person I was all along?

After all, at the end of the day...
All in all, all is all there is,
because all is all I have to give.

From My End...

Different moments were captured by these eyes, saved by this mind, felt by this heart and soul.

Various moments of the good and bad times, this mind defines creativity, releasing pure honesty from this heart and soul.

The Bipolar Charge (Intro)

Half of me is comfortable,
the other half is close to the edge.

Part of me wants to be in love,
the other part just wants
a woman in my bed.

A third of my heart is loaded
with passion, the rest is still
recovering from an
emotional laceration.

I'm positively charged by
an ambitious soul.

Once in a while I'm shocked
by negativity, then this causes
my mind to take a stroll.

Sober Underneath the LED Lights
(In My Room)

When I sleep, my mind often gets away from me. If you only knew what my subconscious really shows me.

I'm ripe with pain, but I know where my heart needs to be. One vacancy for someone to make me feel complete.

Some know how I feel about love, but is it designed for me? Some strongly believe, it's out there waiting for me.

My love is strong, I will never
find another love with such potency.
There will be one woman that will
find out, just wait and see.

I know you're out there, a soulful
being that is designed for me.
With an effervescent personality,
that will accept me for being me.

The Pregame (Introspection)

Riding in the back of a friend's
Duramax,
sitting highly relaxed,
as this Whiskey and coke
course through my veins.

On the outside I'm fine, but inside
thoughts harvest within my domain.
Time and time again,
I've done my best to maintain.
It seems this liquor is opening up
a certain door with a weird wood stain.

Behind this door, there is a
residue of emptiness.
This room has been
cleared out several times.

It was last filled with great memories
of a woman I was in love with.
For years I've refrained from
certain inquiries of why...

Behind the scenes,
a part of me wants a
woman to fill in this space.

The other part of me feels
like I'm going to be single
forever, because I'm afraid
of letting someone in.

Drunk Underneath The Flashing Lights (The Wharf)

As this liquor removes my filter,
I begin to verbalize sweet nothings
to a woman I barely know.
As we dance all night,
she gives me an invite to
come back to her place.

Should I go home to nothing,
and daydream about this
woman I really adore.

Or give in to this woman,
that will only give me half
of her love behind a closed door.
I want to give in to this feeling,
I can't let lust get the better of me.

But this single life isn't what it seems to be,

I often imagine letting a woman get closer.

An amazing woman that is good for me…

So, if I give in to the pressure,

I'll only be using this woman to

fill this hole in my heart temporarily.

Episodes IV

Someone uttered a particular word;
thoughts have begun to flow.
Self-destruction comes attached
with the influence of selling your soul.
Loading a connection with my
heart of gold and this bruised soul.
Sociable drink, gripping the glass,
trying to distill my soul.

Searching for a euphoria of success,
has become my life's goal.
Lost in this drift of a lost episode,
so away we go.

Someone once uttered, my struggle
is a blessing in disguise.
Pulling the trigger on past events,
causing my chances of happiness to downsize.
Blowing things out of proportion,

my mind tends to tick counterclockwise.
Flashbacks that are memorized,
with other thoughts I still idealize.
Could life be greener on the other side,
or a deadly sin in disguise?
Poetic exercise opens rooms of
improvement to help me compromise.

Writing down my feelings could
be an emotional sacrifice.
Good man with a broken heart,
with flaws that are recognized.

In search of opportunity,
my known fears aren't far behind.
Life is what you make of it;
my mortal mind is on the borderline.
Fixated on individual happiness,
this is probably why my love is blind.
Isolating myself daily,
asking God to give me a sign.

The Aftermath IV

So much has happened to me.
Heart breaks, a fair share of
eviction notices and times where
I went to sleep without eating.
I could touch basis on this,
page after page, but we
all must go through it...
That's the adversity
we must face in this life;
I'm not alone in this struggle.

My last heart break was
really bad, because I loved
her...I really loved her.

That's a poem for
another book, maybe!!!
If this book does really well...

Anyway, times got really hard,
I had to break my lease on
my apartment in Shreveport
and move back home to Lake Charles.
When I moved back, I was
really disappointed in myself,
I left all my friends behind.
I felt like I abandoned
them and my Godchildren.

This book you're reading wasn't
in the works, it was only an idea.
I entered three poems in
three poetry contests, just to
see if I really was as good
as others said I was.
I didn't win any of the contests,
but all three poems were published.

I really needed/wanted the money.
I gained a little confidence
over that period of time,
until I found out one of my
childhood best friends took his own life.

That's when I took my book idea seriously!
I just felt like I could've helped
him emotionally and mentally.

Feeding Your Mental Appetite IV

Without the past, there
would be nothing to
think about, let alone
someone to think it.

Without the present, there
would never be a moment
to define, let alone
someone to cherish it.

Without the future, there
would be nothing to
look forward to, let alone
someone to dream it.

If you think about your past,
then in that present moment
defines your next move, while moving
toward a bright future.

True Beauty of Time

Time after time, time and again,
time and time again,
Supposedly, I have all the time
in the world, but I still don't
know where to begin.
We feel there's not
enough time in a day.

Time is slow, when you're
waiting for a special day to arrive.
Even when you're ready to
get off work, or better yet
when you're ready for
a bad day to be over with.

Time flies, even when you're enjoying
a special moment with someone.
Supposedly, it also flies
when a bill is due,

even when it feels like you
just paid it a week ago.

Time becomes precious,
especially when you want
to spend it with someone
special.
Even when you want
to give a person all your love.
It often becomes a
great value when you want to
make up for lost time.

Time is often wasted,
when you sit there in self-pity.
Even when you just want
to give up or procrastinate.
Especially when chasing a
man/woman that
has no interest in you.

Time heals all wounds when
you dwell upon euphoric
surroundings of friendship.
Because the moment you
let that positivity in, then
the healing process begins.
As time goes by,
I've learned the true beauty of it.
It's not about how much
time you put in, it's about
what you put in the time.
I've spent countless hours
trying to hone in on this craft.

Time waits for no one…
The clock is ticking and
my time is now.

The question now is,
"What are you going to do
with the time on your hands?"

Some will scroll through the newsfeed,
 share some video or picture
followed by hashtag relationship goals;
when it really starts with communication.
 Create a new recipe of friendship,
 relationship, and partnership.
 Open up to someone that shows
 signs of 'foreverness.'
Don't follow the types of men/women that trend;
 focus on creating a longevity of real love...

Mark My Words

I found a way to channel
this negativity in my heart.

Words play softly in my mind
like a violin in the dark.

I promise to raise the bar
and I let honesty play its part.

Who knew I would be so
addicted to this branch of art.

I won't live forever, but in each
poem is where I leave my mark.

Building Some Self-Confidence

If you are reading this...

Well.... Just know I want to be

the greatest poet dead or alive

To be continued...

Meanwhile....

As some stress themselves

to fit in or live up to an image,

meanwhile in Louisiana,

I'm mapping myself out

to become a rare legend.

To All Of The Poets....

When you think a poem doesn't make sense; post it anyway, because someone will make sense of it...

Mind Racing

Sitting here in privacy,
reflecting on my past and this society,
as this iPhone harnesses my
emotional energy and creativity.

Every moment I wonder, if everything
I fancy is in another dimension.
A lot of wants and needs, but the
wants are outweighing my needs.

Every day I stare at this publication form.
Lost in reverie; pleasant thoughts
of my book with an incredible outcome.

I'm just a poet that's trying to
connect with my readers.
Spending most of my time trying
to hone this literature skill.
Some of that time is used in

understanding words, I can't pronounce,
along with every ounce of my being,
to help you feel what I'm feeling.

I remember so much of my life
thus far, I often reenact memories.
I be the poem just to let you
know, I'm hurting with you.
While giving my readers food
for thought, as my organic
thoughts give them mental fiber,
that could help them digest stress,
and worries that their brain
and heart don't need.

Beyond this fleshy surface,
I ponder about my true purpose,
wondering if I'm built for something special.

As I grow, I still stare in the mirror,
and I still often question my identity.
I express my point of views.
That's what makes me
unique as a poet.
I'm not perfect, but I'm here
if you need encouragement.

I'm often caught in ambitious
cogitations about this society;

So many people of all races
with different faces,
have the same euphoric ambition.

Deep in my heart,
I know we're all equal...

We all have our struggles,
problems, trials and tribulations,
along with hopes of happiness.

It seems like ignorance is contagious,
people living to react.

Daydreaming of ways to make
this world a better place,
but I'm just a small detail
trying to make a difference.
I'm only one man trying to
alleviate the moral mind from
depressions, anxiety, etc.

All lives matter to me,
every time I type these emotions in this iPhone.
We are all human.
Various things disconnect, separate,
classify and divide us.

Why can't we step back for a
second and understand?
Before you point a finger
at someone, look in the mirror,

and point a finger at yourself,
because you might be
part of the problem.
At the end of the day, if we
try to get rid of a small portion
of ignorance, some will realize that
love can keep us together.

I'm just a man with my
own problems and big
ambitions, in search for
greatness, romance and love.
I'm woolgathering, my heart pacing,
my mind racing,
about what we're facing.

This world will become
a better place, the moment
we realize that working and staying
together will be the moment we rise.

Downloading Heavenly Strength

All I have in this world is pockets full of hope,
an iPhone full of poems and walking on a tightrope.

Facing life without an unpleasant behavior,
is walking between success and failure.
I'm broke, online searching for good paying jobs,
losing patience, but this heart calmly throbs.

I daydream of making it, I need some insight…
Steady brimming with ideas, so much to write…
Emotional gumbo with a smell of erudite…

With several raw potent ingredients,
along with a pure soul and heart for balance.
At times I let it set in, time is of the essence.
I used to burn the roux of some of my poems' ideas;
I take my time, letting my feelings cook slowly.

I'm possible for doing the impossible
as long as I give all I possibly can.
Opportunity is somewhere out there;
I refuse to just stand around.

I must keep in mind without struggle
I would never have made this change.
I'm certain there will be better days ahead,
every day of my life I will embrace this change.

Been on this long road accumulating wisdom…
As time proceeds, I want to know everything,
I just want my life to count for something.
This is my life and I refuse to lose custody.

I can do all things through Christ
which strengtheneth me.
[Philippians 4:13] KJV

Give It to God

My mind is bloated,
I need these thoughts to digest.

So much is happening,
I feel like I'm not giving my best.

Seems like when I go east,
I only end up going west.
Look in the back of my mind,
you'll see a hint of fear.
Afraid of failing,
my focus isn't crystal clear.

Trying to take a chance,
I can only live this life once.
Trying to stay strong,
I've been through the
motions of depression once.

We live, and we learn
or we crash, and we burn,
with happiness as our main concern.
I promise to give my all when it's my turn.

Lord forgive me,
there are things in this life I don't understand.
The moment I sit alone I become a pessimist,
but could you give me a better plan?

God, can you hear me praying from so far away?...
Give me the will, the motivation,
the dedication and the strength.

With all the problems that
I'm going through...
I promise to keep moving
and give it all to you....

Tuning In (Intro)

I feel we will all have our dark times.

Moments when we will lose focus.
Moments when we will feel determination
and confidence drifting away.

Certain circumstances will knock us off track.
Stress will sometimes set in and linger.

Sometimes you just need something
to help you go above and beyond.

Till this day, I feel like music can motivate...

Taking you to a better place mentally,
while feeding the soul, harmonious sounds.

Beats by Dre Effect

As the longitudinal wave detaches;
the rhythm, harmony and melody dances,
followed by the 808s as it advances;
creativity swiftly builds and enhances.

As every musical note and lyric relaxes;
freely redecorating my mental canvas,
collecting memories from my mental branches;
even resurrection memories from the ashes.
Jumping to new heights as motivation flashes,
nodding my head, as this calm feeling passes.
Helping me elude from certain circumstances;
altering my moral, avoiding impulsive tantrums
lost in preparation, often searching for answers
deep in my soul, I wait for opportune chances.

A few selected songs have become my anthems,
these headphones stimulate my mind
whenever my determination collapses.

A Grudge That Was Living Rent Free, Pt. 1

My past fuels me to stay, driven to see a brighter future.

Most of my drive comes from wanting to show the women that broke my heart my worth.

But here's where I kick this grudge to the curb, before I end up becoming the villain.

No Hidden Fees

I want those new Retro Jordan 11 "Space Jams,"
but I know that's not me.
Honestly, materialistic things will
never physically or mentally shape me.

There's no point in me wearing twenty-five
percent of my rent on my feet.
They're good for saying I own them.
They won't add any attributes toward me.

You see, no amount of money
can really help me find me.
Money doesn't allow me
to go above and beyond.

How could I ever think a pair of shoes
and my needs should ever correspond?

I have a dollar and a dream,
along with trying to make sense of everything.

Pain has given me wisdom and knowledge,
helping me amount to something.
Every item comes with a price, state/federal tax,
and shipping and handling fees.

My heart and soul come free, with deep
ridiculous passion and no hidden fees.

The Company I Keep

I surround myself with company,
that wants to spread love.

I surround myself with company,
that wants to move forward.
I surround myself with company,
that motivates me.

I surround myself with company,
that helps me make right choices.
I surround myself with company,
that keeps my heart in the right place.

I surround myself with company,
that brings me great joy.

I surround myself with company,
that helps me obtain great knowledge.

I surround myself with company that
accepts me for who I am.

I surround myself with company that do not judge me
for the color of my skin, but for my unselfish actions.

The company I keep, wants to see
me succeed at the highest level.

The company I keep,
helps me appreciate life for what it is.

The company I keep, helps me
understand what life really is about.

To the company I've kept over
the years, thank you for the
inspiration and God bless.

750mg of Honesty and a Proprietary Blend [750 mg of Honesty]

Everyone was worried about the presidential race.

What I'm worried about is how can I get my life back in the right place.

I'm trying to focus on what's really important; right now, my mind feels really distorted.

Some days I search for strength just to get out of bed. I can be a worrywart sometimes; some thoughts will be left unsaid.

Over the years I've put myself in certain predicaments.

When I was flustered, running away
was one of my strategic movements.
Now I face my problems head on,
it took a few emotional adjustments.
Every day I beat myself up;
I just feel like I deserve more.
I'm unsure about my every move;
there's a life I'm trying to restore.

Often at times, I feel so alone…
At night, I hold my pillow very close,
then my mind cast me in a movie role.

A year ago, my confidence
was at an all-time low.
I will never have the confidence to
let my friends and family know.
Sometimes I can be an outcast that likes
to hear music from a speaker box; digging
deep, searching for the love below.

I rather dwell in introspection,

take my time to let poetry know.

Besides, this is how I let my past go,

while letting raw creativity flow.

As I let these emotions go,

I've found a voluminous

amount of space to grow.

I've learned this world can

make you laugh and make you cry.

I refuse to be damaged

by this world.

I refuse to be part of the netherworld.

I write about certain emotions

like that's my department.

I'm doing my best to make every

reader think about life, so they

can play a big part in it.

Everyone goes through stress;

some just want to end it.

Whenever confidence breaks down;
I wonder if I can help them mend it?

I know when you're at the bottom,
down on your luck; dying will always
sound better than living.

I once had a vendetta with the guy
in the mirror.
I even blamed God for
the cards I was given.

Stress is stress, pain is pain,
no matter how it's given.
Some will make it seem like
you don't know their pain.
At the end of the day, some of
us will ask the same questions,
looking for the same answers.

Face it, you will never be mentally

prepared for every situation.
The moment you dwell in that
negative rumination, that's when
doubt can stain your determination.
I remember the moments when negativity
would set in and fill me with doubt.
Back then I was doing my best to fit in,
but I've realized, I'm pre-destined to stand out.

My past can fuel a bright future,
with every step I find myself eager.
I'm still a bit scared about
what the future holds.
I think about how much
of an impact my words will hold.
Some nights I lay in my bed and
wonder how close I am to greatness.
If I'm not close enough;
I'm going to have to create
my own path, so excuse
me for my lateness.

[Proprietary Blend]

I think my mother is worried
that I will be single forever.
I'm somewhat a nonbeliever
of genuine love; however,
I'm somewhat mentally prepared
to be great with or without someone in my corner.

Most women would put that
potential man in the friend zone.
Then come back to him temporarily
when their heart needs a home.
When they find that so-called potential man again,
they will leave that crutch at home.

Some do this selfish act just
to feel comfort from someone.
Some will complain how a good
man is really hard to find.

Meanwhile she is in your arms, not
knowing you're the man she can't find.
As you hug her in the back of your mind,
you're wishing your love could keep her here.
You're not looking for sex, you want to give
all of your heart to a noble compeer.
Instead you end up giving your love
towards someone that won't stay near.

These days I can be a little anti-social.
Sometimes I don't feel available emotionally.
Without a woman I've realized
some feelings are heightened.
Maybe I'm single because,
I love a little bit differently.
I will always do more than what you ask of me.
For years I've held a grudge
against certain women.

Some cried to me, some begged
me to take them back.
Some try to rebuild our friendship,
to gain my trust back.
Some didn't want a relationship,
some just want a sex-ship.
Some wanted to know my occupation,
then realized I wasn't stable financially.
Some said I'm a great man,
a few said I was too perfect.

Some wanted to see a change,
but not be present for it.

Many will never understand genuine love;
I often imagine how would
it feel, just to feel that.

I believe some genuine love is lost,
just not on my end.

Feeding Your Mental Appetite V

When someone positively thinks more of you…

Take a moment of introspection,

to search for the very essence

of your true potential.

Plant yourself in that very area of your mind,

when you bloom,

you will notice a better you.

Other acquaintances will take notice,

and admire that bloom of confidence.

I think more of you,

take a moment…

You are worth more than you think.

So, Any Questions?

Any questions you want to ask, just ask...
I'm not looking to chase tail, I want love.
If you're not looking for love, I get it...
Friends it is then....
Every woman I've ever met with or without kids,
say they don't want anything serious. You're working
on yourself, I get it on every level of life.
I found myself as a man,
we are all capable of great things.
I don't play games, I don't make excuses.
I'm not like any other man, you have ever met.
I've built myself to be a better man.
You don't have to believe me.
If you read my poems, my only goal is to make
someone smile, while making them feel complete.
I'm not trying to be the person that will stress you out,
I'm trying to be the person that makes you smile
in every aspect of your life.
I'm not crazy, I'm just being me.

My Practice

My mind, body, and soul
has been through so much. I know,
I'm not the only one.
There are other people that are in
worse circumstances.
I was afraid of writing about
things that were on my mind.
I was afraid of being judged.

I don't write this closure for your sympathy.
I write this closure, only to help some
realize their blessings, and help others get over
that threshold of emotions, that may plague them.

I'm not better than you, I'm in the same boat as you.

I'm just sacrificing my thoughts
to save others like you.

Compathy: Session V

We all have deep emotional secrets, the feeling of being embarrassed, having a deep fear of something, it could be someone we love or like. There are so many other deep emotional secrets, but I have all three of those deep emotional secrets.

A part of me feels embarrassed/ashamed about my position in life. I often hear others say I'm a great guy, I would be a great husband, I'll be a great father, etc., etc., and etc. These are the deepest fears others have imprinted in my head so far, but in the back

of my mind I really want

to know if it's all true.

I have at least three women

I would love to be with.

I've taken their pulchritude

from my point of view.

To not only tell them how I feel,

but what I see, and what I think of them.

Also give them confidence

and display to other women,

that there are men out there that

just want one woman to

be the brightest star in their galaxy.

They may not write like this or be as clever with words.

They're watching, wondering and

wishing for that chance.

Finding a way to

get your attention.

Yearning for That Moment

I know a handful of words from dictionary.com.

I often sweven about showing a significant other the true meaning of only one.

My subconscious knows the phrase I'm dying to hear.

I'm such a sucker for love.
I would love, love till it
avoids or resents me.
Love could be
a beautiful stranger,
I would even love
who it pretends to be...

Cherishing the Fragmented Pieces

In this world certain people
will bamboozle you,
harm you emotionally,
even break you down.

No matter how broken up you are,
or how emotionally scarred you are,
I'm willing to take you as you are.

I'm here to help mend the pieces.

I don't want these few fragmented
pieces of you.

I want the whole thing.

A Portrait of Unity (Intro)

As your eyes capture
pulchritude or handsomeness,
put in consideration of the inner
beauty of that person,
physical attractiveness can only
go so far...

Admire the personality,
the politeness, the integrity,
the intelligence, the wisdom
and charisma.

You should display
your actions like an artist with
a meaningful passion that takes his/her
time to bring out the unity within that piece.

Portrait of a Woman

A spontaneous idea strikes in this brainstorm;
a way of capturing a woman in organic form.

A painting with a twist, that should make
every man appreciates true bliss.

Eleven by fourteen sheet with a vellum finish;
acid-free so this artwork will never diminish.

Thinking of poses, shape and size;
I want her to feel beauteous, pint-size or full-size.

A rough sketch shows curves and
edges of her identity;
every detail will show great unity.

As curve lines capture euphoria in disguise,
while circles display the integrity in her eyes.

Inner U's, a few arch lines will be worthwhile,
as I go the extra mile just to make her smile.

With every touch of my HB pencil,
I begin to unlock her true potential.

With a blending stump, I add shades of value;
time is well spent as I appreciate her true value.

A kneaded eraser, attempting to erase her fear,
while making emotional smudges disappear.
Every line has seized this precious moment;
strong complementary acts of color will hold it.

I don't care about her skin color; any tone will
show visual satisfaction of harmony and luster.
Yet her physical attractiveness is beauteous,
the mixture of her inner beauty is marvelous.

As I step back to admire the complete balance;
I did right by giving her a positive influence.

Beauty is what you make it; I've taken extra
time to make her look and feel confident.
There may be other copies of women,
but it's nothing like the original,
I've put my time in.

The Iris Effect

If you were to stare into her blue eyes,
you may feel an oasis of calm.

Soaked in a specific ocean,
where stress would be diluted,
a wave of eudaemonia would gently,
brush over you from this ocean current.

A personality that's like a
breath of fresh air,
that adds eight knots under your sail.

As you propel through this current, you
will experience a journey of a life time.

Encore

I've noticed her lows, her highs.
She does what she can, just to get by.

I see the lack of excitement,
her soul lays dormant
without accompaniment.

I only want to orchestrate
an emotional performance.

A composing effect to be
the music to her soul.

She is the only spectator
I want to yell out... ENCORE!!!

Wiping Away Her Tears...

She's been hurt by a recent event.

I can hear her heart crying out for comfort.
I understand we will have our bad days.

I'm used to seeing her laughing and smiling.
I'm accustomed to her bouncy personality.

As I feel her heart residing to sadness.
I wish my hugs can comfort her with a
ray of sunshine, along with alleviating
her sadness with playful banter.

I just want to wipe away her tears...

Just to bring back her bouncy personality,
and see that angelic smile once again.

A Senseless Flower of Remembrance I

I want the very essence
of this senseless flower,
to remind you of the extract
of purity and essential
innocence of your very soul.
When you gaze upon this flower,
take a moment to let this medium softly;
awaken your gentle and subtle nature.
May it ease whatever harsh experiences
your heart and mind may encounter.
Stay positive, stand tall and
blossom where you are planted...

Heart of Gold

I want my words to be
like a soft-bristle brush.
Removing dirt lodged
in every nook and cranny.

I want my actions to be
like a soft cloth,
that polishes your heart of gold.

From a distance, I've observed
this woman from my perspective.
I hear she's high maintenance,
I think she's searching for perfection.
Make up doesn't cover up imperfections,
"What is she searching for?" is my question.
My love doesn't hit her;
I want to keep her safe.
My love doesn't come with a price,
because it is priceless.
My love isn't cold, because I will
take the time to keep her warm.
My love isn't ordinary, because
I'll take the time to make her feel special.
Love is kind, but my love is one of a kind,
that could make a diamond like her shine.

She catches me staring at her quite often…
Quite often, I'm wondering if I'm even an option.
I wonder if she wonders about me; am I even a topic?
Maybe she has a list, but am I on the top of it?
Does she put me in heartfelt euphoric scenarios?
Euphoric scenarios… I have tons of those.
Becoming one with her mind, body and soul.
I just want our love to be a sight to behold.

The Inception of a Beauteous Universe

If I told you I could inspire your lost soul,
would you leave that negative boundary of your mind
so, I can help you find an emotional sense of identity?
From in the depths of my soul,
I sense something special inside of you.
If I shed a value of light on the shade of your doubt;
would you trust me with your broken heart?

I can help fill in the missing pieces.
From in the depths of my soul,
I sense a beauteous universe inside of you.
If I color you with a priceless value of confidence,
erasing the fears of being lost,
would you take my hand as we take a journey
to the positive boundary of your mind?

I bet you never even knew, you had a beauteous universe inside of you.

What Love May Bring...

No one's around to influence us with negativity.

You be yourself and I'll be me.

Let love start here, let love stay here.

For a moment, let love flow free.

Let's go to a place where our hearts can only find...

Close your eyes, slowly embrace

the meaningful silence.

With no thought of letting go,

let's accept what love may bring.

Can I Just Be Honest I

The last time you were around,
I was trying not to stare your way.
Sometimes I get butterflies,
because there's a scenario
I play in my head over and over.

I finally get to hold you close,
placing my forehead against yours,
staring into your eyes,
rubbing my lips against yours,
teasing you before the action occurs.

Then you clinch my shirt
and pull me in closer.
Time itself freezes,
for a brief moment,
as if someone wanted us
to cherish this very moment.

We kiss and for that moment
I feel so alive, but I come to
realize my surroundings.

I shake my head from
left to right, trying to shake
off these thoughts and butterflies.

I respect you and I would
never do anything to hurt you,
I will do everything to inspire you…

A Senseless Flower of Remembrance II

The very essence of
this single senseless rose bud
has a deep sentiment.

I see the growth of great
potential, the loveliness,
even the purity in your heart.

I even want to acknowledge the
great admiration I have for you.
I'm reaching out to you,
because of the inner beauty
that needs to be released.

Unlock the courage within,
and never accept defeat.
I hope this rose bud reminds you,
that you possess great potential.

This rose bud will never boast
about what it's capable of,
it will only take action and blossom.

The Main Ingredient

I'll occupy your time;
when you feel alone.

I'll lift you up;
when you're feeling down.

I'll latch onto you;
when you're feeling scared.

I'll lend you my ear;
when you need to vent.

I'll make you feel beauteous;
when you're not wearing makeup.

I'll break down the
boundaries of negativity,
and surround you with positivity.

I want to be that man,

that makes you smile, even

when I walk into a room.

When I have you in my space,

I promise I won't let go of you.

I want my love to be the main ingredient

that makes you feel complete.

The Imaginings in My Head

If I could snap my fingers;
changing us into formal attire,
transforming the area around us,
the sky is dark, the stars are
illuminating bright, the moon
shines on us like a spotlight.

Could I carefully take you by the hand,
shining the spotlight on
the great wonders of my mindset?
We'd dance all night beneath the stars
creating our soundtrack with the
soulful melodies in our hearts.
I'd spin you in to my arms,
as we seal this moment with a kiss.

Your breath is slowly taken away,
then you exhale as if you had to get
accustomed to this new atmosphere of love.

Queen of Hearts

If the cards of life could
 be dealt differently;

  you would be
  the only queen
 I would want in my grasp.

An Eyeful of Pulchritude (Intro)

As I exchange messages
with her on Instagram,
I get slightly trapped in
a wave of nostalgia.

I go to her profile, then
scroll through each picture.

My scenarios become a love
story that hasn't even been written yet.
A picture can be expressed with so many words,
I've thought of a thousand plus more.

I admit, I ogle over each picture,
but she deserves every ounce of respect.
As these pictures capture her at every angle,
my curiosity is set on experiencing
every detail of her personality.

As I Admire Her Instagram Photos

She gets at least a hundred plus likes...

Along with comments of
beautiful, gorgeous,
sexy, hot,
even the emoji with hearted eyes.

If I comment
beauteous, radiant, comely, ravishing,
would it come as a surprise?

I know she probably receives
all kinds of weird or disgusting messages
in her DM (direct messages).

She's so filled with pulchritude...
How can I express,
"I'm nothing like them?"

The Message I Want to Send

You're the main ingredient
that adds flavor, to the
imaginings in my head.

You're the only queen I want in my grasp.
The portrait of a woman,
I will always adore.

I would like to take you
on a very romantic date.
And let the attraction
appear and take shape.
If there's any chance,
I have no problem
taking time out of my schedule.

If not, at the end of the day,
at least I can say "I tried."

Just a Moment of Your Time...

Just hug me
for twenty seconds
and release your serotonin.

As my physical presence
sets aside stress and
let well-being tune in.

Let's zone out, then hone in,
the feeling
that our hearts are holding.

iOS Love Update

I don't want
to steal your heart…

I want

to enhance it,

better yet

update it

every so often.

Just to let you know,

my love for you

is up to date.

Somehow, he can see
her loving heart,
but he rather remain in the dark.
How would we know
that it's really love?
How would it start?
We have no sign of this possibility,
but we both can wield the ability.
Would she open up,
and let him display love
with every heartbeat?
Defeat the negativity
that often creeps,
and makes her weak,
just to make her
feel complete.

If You Ever Want Real Love...

I've realized you're searching for
answers in an abstract painting.

Often picturing yourself,
with a man with money
and various materialistic things
to impress you.

The picture I've painted
is impressively detailed.

My love will never go out of style.
Designer clothes, heels, make up,
will never make you feel as beauteous
as my love will.
Different transportation
will never take you to a place,
where my love will take you.

In the lonely hour, when the darkness
begins to shade you and your doubt,
money and various materialistic
things will never love you like I can.

I'm not God's gift to women,
I only want to present my love
in its genuine state.

I'll cherish your love.
You deserve to be appreciated,
like the flawless gem you are.
If you ever want real love, you know
where to find the rarest extract.

She takes selfies,
then posts them for the whole world
to see.
Deep down inside,
she wants the attention
of only one man.
With so many likes and comments
how could she ever find...the "one?"
How could he ever connect to
her Wi-Fi with no password?

Hopefully One Day...

When the time comes,
I want to write a poem just for you.
In the purest extract of honesty,
confessing how I really feel about you.
No one knows exactly who you are;
even you don't have a clue.

Staring at your profile,
some of these poems are about you.
Looking for love on social media,
I can't stop thinking of you.

Feeling ashamed,
wishing your love was something
I could claim.
If you only knew,
I've always had imprinted
thoughts of you in my brain.

I picture us together
like a camera phone would;
with no reason to adjust the resolution.
Behind the scenes are a high level
of intense mental cardio,
with previous record videos
of long scenarios
with high-def audio.

My curious hands want to
smooth out the tension,
in every nook and cranny
of your every curve.
No words are verbally
served, only actions
that physically make my
syllables of my verbs curve.
As I spread comfort all
over your stressful body,
I pull you close to indicate,
that I am the one you deserve.

The Mirror Dimension

In the end I must confess;
I love you.
I've spent countless hours
analyzing every aspect of you.
From the way you carry yourself to
hearing your laugh from a distance.

You will read this and assume...
If I speak of you or some other...
You may text me in search
for the correct answer.

This will be an unsolved mystery,
a hidden thought that will
probably stay with me.
Curiosity has driven me to
build castles in the air.

I wish I could take time to
meet with you in the mirror
dimension and converse with you.

Reshaping the beauty of romance
without fear of adversely affecting
the natural order of real love.

You know nothing about love,
if you don't understand the beauty of it.

In all honesty... I've been doubting
myself on this book...
I ask myself over and over,
"Who would take time
out to purchase this book?
Will it touch readers
the way I want it to?"
Then I doubt my writing,
some of my poems in general...
BUT... I never stopped writing;
I owe it to myself.
I've given up once in life
and I will not do it again.

I write poetry, because it
does something to me.
I love the atmosphere.
It allows me to breathe in.
When I'm in that element
I feel every emotion, and
I can control it...every moment.
I feel like there's someone
that needs to feel confident,
someone that needs wisdom,
someone that just needs to know
that they are not alone
in this struggle we call life.
Even a woman that
needs to feel beauteous.
I can do all of that with poetry
while giving you a glimpse
of my world...
So, with the awards I've received
I take a strong stride forward...

THANK YOU FOR YOUR SUPPORT...

Appreciate a person's heart, trust, and loyalty, because it doesn't come with a life-time warranty…

I don't want to hesitate
on giving up my love;
I just want to break down
and give it all away…

Everything starts
with an inspirational rush,
next the ideas emerge.
Then creativity takes over
with scenarios of wishful hope.
Passion grows,
and proceeds to amplify
the mental capacity
ten times over.

From: All Four Chambers
To: Kayleigh & Jaxsen (My Godchildren)

I wish, I was around you more,

so, I can watch you grow.

Over the years you've taught

me so much.

Your love always came

in the clutch.

When you're around

a different part of me triggers.

I've never thought of myself

as a father figure,

a role model maybe.

I'll always look at you as if

you were one of my own.

You've helped me find the

best vision of myself.
I want nothing more,
but to only see you succeed.
You make me feel so alive.
You've added so much
meaning to my life.
As these emotions disperse
with such precision,
at the end of the day,
you've saved my life.

At the end of the day, I learned
the values of a father.

Since I've moved back to Lake Charles, La,
I feel like I'm missing everything.
I loved spending every moment with you,
and my biggest fear is losing your love.

I love you with
all four chambers of my heart.
I cherish you more
than any valuable jewel.
I not only want to be great,
I want to be great to you.

You always alleviated
whatever stress I was facing.
You are truly a blessing...
You're another reason why
I believe in this life...

If you don't know what's
going on in your life;
re-evaluate your surroundings.
Find a different atmosphere that
can sustain the life you really want.
Set goals that can
be accomplished and
accomplish them.

I was once uncomfortable
about who I was becoming.
It felt like I was trying
to be someone else.
I was ashamed,
even afraid of being myself,
because of the problems I was facing.
The moment I gained the courage to be myself,
was the moment I found myself.
That's the moment I accepted who I am.
I am amazed of the talent I discovered!!
I had no inkling of what I was capable of...
Until I stopped trying to be
what the world wanted me to be.
A conglomeration of events
made me realize my destiny,
now I know who I was born to be.
Be who you are, even when
the world mistakes you for
who they think you are.

*A Conglomeration of Poems,
While I Save Up for My
Publication Deposit...*

Take life for what it's worth
and increase the value of it.

I'm a man with negative and
positive secrets, a past with
hopes of a brighter future,
but in between the neutral
is you and me...
Incorrect thoughts of English,
I'm all for it, how about you.
How would you contribute
to this story in order to
make me feel complete?

Money comes and goes,
real love comes every
once in a while.

If you want to buy someone's heart, it should be at the cost of your trust, love and loyalty.

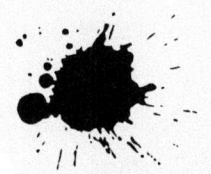

I will never be around my friends,
when I'm trying to solve
my own problems.
I may seem distant,
but I like to take them on by myself...
I'm a wise man, that slowly
swallows his own pride.

So many have put a certain
thought in my head;
that I'm going to become famous,
when I finally release my book.
And somehow, I believe it myself...
But, I keep reminding myself
to never forget where I've come from.

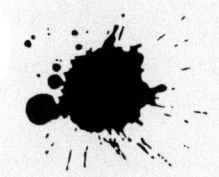

I take in Snapchats of you,
then curiosity commence.
How could I convince my
loyalty with some kind
of positive sense?
I could send emojis for every
picture, but my actions can
start and finish every sentence.

We are only friends,
but deep down inside
I want more.
As each thought comes ashore,
sending nervous
quivers to my inner core.
With every sight of your
physical presence,
I just want you more
and more.
You may care deeply for
someone else,
but I will always
imagine I was all yours.

Pardon the Interruption with Twenty-One Minutes Left

I have twenty-one minutes, before I have to clock-in.
I have time to let my mind flow like a fountain pen.

If you take time to observe your surroundings
you may find something inspiring.
Once you find the deep beauty in something,
take time to be cleverly aspiring.

I frequently think now, rewind...
about an episode that happened
to me way back then.
I'm not a saint, I'm a human being
that knows his share about sin.
Carefully practiced being a gentleman
with a special positive blend.

I'm not better than you, but I'm not like you at all
and I refuse to sit here and pretend.

Anhedonia

I used to wonder, how to move on,
analyzing where I went wrong.
At times I would sit and cry,
wishing I could live with no fear.
I was so down and out, now I use
poetry to shed my every tear.
With a poor appetite, bills and
hopes of having one great year.

I'm an affectionate gent with goals of
being a long-term worthy resident.
With the development of loyalty,
as I help one woman harness love
in its true element.

All I ever tried to do is be relevant;
with evidence that my love is definite.
(To Be Continued...)

You're the thought I
can't shake away,
each and every day…
You're the one thought
that stays at bay.
You're the thought
that never folds,
the thought I always miss.
You're the thought
I want to hold,
I want to kiss.
You're the thought
they claim as a myth,
the thought I want to
spend my life with.

At one point in my life,
I really wanted to sell my soul.
I wanted money, cars, clothes,
woman, and every expensive
thing that was ever sold.
But... One day I discovered
the true meaning of life,
because the other stuff
will never make me whole.

Sometimes you will embrace
the hopes of love,
instead of embracing the true nature of it.

I've experienced, puppy love.
I've experienced, playing with love.
I've experienced, not wanting to
receive someone's love.
I've experienced, getting hurt by love.
I've experienced, the process of
trying to understand love.
I've experienced, being a sucker for love.
I've experienced, giving my love all at once.
I've experienced, fearing love.
I've experienced, accepting love,
while getting mentally prepared
for the pain that it can cause.
I've experienced, the process of
digging deep just to write about love.
I've experienced, seeing love
in its purest form.
I've experienced,
the real reason why love is blind.
I've experienced, seeing
true love, during a marriage.
I've experienced,
not feeling love or
not being noticed by it.
I've experienced, the amount
of love a child can have for you.

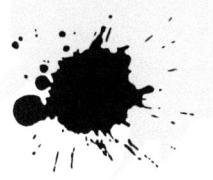

My thoughts of you are often,
interrupted by the labors of my job.
But... I find my way back to you,
mentally.

I know I'm not your significant other,
but I catch myself making plans;
as if you were already mine.

Melatonin Chronicles II

Resting my forehead against hers,
closing my eyes as
the feelings I'm hiding arrive.

She tightly clinches
my tri-blend shirt,
as she feels the emotional drive.
I take a deep breath,
before this kiss sends my heart in overdrive.

Statements coated with all truth and no lies.
Uniting for one purpose,
becoming emotional allies.

Capitalizing on this feeling
that has made us come alive.

Embracing this moment, bringing
life to a feeling that will survive.

Sometimes the potential
significant other is right there.
But... How can you display
actions that indicate,
that you are the right person for them?
There's no crystal ball for
you to show them the future
of your loyalty, personality,
the politeness, the integrity,
the intelligence, the wisdom,
the charisma and love.
I feel like love is a shot in the dark;
but when the two meet,
both will shine brighter than the stars
with the means of making sure,
their light never dims.

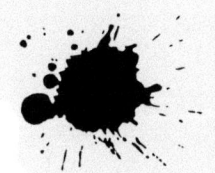

Fiend for a relationship that's rich;
not for someone that is rich....
Materialistic things won't help
you marinate in euphoria.
Stop digging for ideal gold,
instead find someone special to hold;
love is made not sold.

I would love to love you, but
something is holding you back.

Love shouldn't come equipped with mind games.

Gin and Tonic with a Freshly Cut Lime

I'm sipping on this gin and tonic,
with a freshly cut lime.
Pondering about the time,
when you were mine.

I know if I text you, you will
never take the time to reply.
If you want to be with me,
hurry up and make up your mind.
I feel demoralized, without
having any kind of a sign.

I still scroll through
these old text messages.
A source of reference that
comes along with vivid images.
Musing about how we

use to feel;

everything that was said... was it real?

It came along with well

deserved love that was real.

Now I'm gathering every sheet

of my thoughts;

slipping it in to an envelope with a self-seal.

When I feel like I'm using a woman,
I stray away before I do more damage.
I know how it feels to be used,
and what kind of damage can be done.
But in some cases, some of us
would rather be used;
just to feel some form of emotion,
rather than to feel nothing at all...

We will love a person
that will disappoint us,
and we will also disappoint
a person that will love us.

At the end of the day;
I just want to be with a
significant other that
truly knows my value…

Hidden Agenda

Someone will try to give you their love,
but you will have
hidden feelings to give
your love to another.

Meanwhile, as you will try to give
your love to that other,
they may have a hidden agenda
to find someone
with a meaningless standard
that could make their life better.

www.ingramcontent.com/pod-product-compliance
Lightning Source LLC
Chambersburg PA
CBHW041351290426
44108CB00001B/7